HISTORY'S VILLAINS

BLOODY MARY

DISCARD

Louise Chipley Slavicek

BLACKBIRCH PRESS

An imprint of Thomson Gale, a part of The Thomson Corporation

THOMSON

★

GALE

Detroit • New York • S • Munich

THOMSON

GALE

LIBRARY OF CONGRESS CATALOGING-IN-PUBLICATION DATA

Slavicek, Louise Chipley, 1956-
  Bloody Mary / by Louise Chipley Slavicek.
     p. cm. — (History's villains)
  Includes bibliographical references and index.
  ISBN 1-4103-0581-3 (alk. paper)
  1. Mary I, Queen of England, 1516–1558—Juvenile literature. 2. Great Britain—History—Mary I, 1553–1558—Juvenile literature. 3. Queens—Great Britain—Biography—Juvenile literature. I. Title. II. Series.

  DA347.S57 2005
  942.05'4'092—dc22
                                                                2005001830

Printed in the United States of America

CONTENTS

INTRODUCTION: "BLOODY MARY"   5

Chapter 1   THE YOUNG PRINCESS   11

Chapter 2   "THE MOST UNHAPPY LADY IN
            CHRISTENDOM"   30

Chapter 3   MARY'S CHANGING FORTUNES   48

Chapter 4   THE NEW QUEEN   66

Chapter 5   TRAITORS AND HERETICS   83

            CHRONOLOGY   103

            GLOSSARY   105

            SOURCE NOTES   107

            FOR MORE INFORMATION   109

            INDEX   110

            PICTURE CREDITS   112

INTRODUCTION: "BLOODY MARY"

On the morning of October 16, 1555, fifty-four-year-old Nicholas Ridley and seventy-year-old Hugh Latimer were taken to a ditch just outside the town walls of Oxford, England, and chained back-to-back to a single wooden stake. Ridley looked stately in a velvet cap and fur-trimmed black robe, his customary attire as bishop of London. In contrast to Ridley's elegant appearance, elderly Hugh Latimer, the retired bishop of Worcester, was dressed in a simple white linen gown that reminded some onlookers of a burial shroud.

As their executioners piled wood and faggots—small bundles of straw and sticks—around the Protestant clerics' feet and legs, Latimer shouted encouragement to his longtime friend and colleague in the Church of England. "Be of good comfort, Master Ridley, and play the man," Latimer was heard to say. "We shall this day light such a candle, by God's grace, in England, as I

For executing hundreds of Protestants in England, Queen Mary I will forever be known to history as Bloody Mary.

trust shall never be put out."[1] No sooner had Latimer uttered these words than a lighted torch was tossed into the faggots and flames shot up around the men's calves and thighs.

Fortunately for Latimer, the fire on his side of the stake burned fiercely and his suffering was soon over. His friend, however, was not as fortunate. On Ridley's side of the stake, the executioners had piled on the faggots too thickly, and the fire burned with an agonizing slowness. After nearly an hour, the flames had completely burned away the bishop's legs but still had not reached his upper body. Again and again he cried out in his torment, "Let the fire come unto me, I cannot burn."[2] Finally, a sympathetic bailiff pulled some of the higher faggots from the pile with his staff. The fire flamed to Ridley's face and to the immense relief of the horrified onlookers, he stirred no more.

Savior or Villain?

The crime for which Nicholas Ridley and Hugh Latimer had been condemned to suffer such a terrible death that autumn morning in 1555 was heresy: the holding of beliefs that differ from the teachings of the established church. Bishops Ridley and Latimer were just two of nearly three hundred Protestant heretics to be burned alive during the brief reign of Queen Mary I of England (1553–1558). Yet although Mary would go down in history as "Bloody Mary," a religious fanatic of extraordinary cruelty, she saw herself as a savior, not a villain. A devout Roman Catholic from earliest childhood, Mary was dismayed by England's gradual move toward Protestant Christianity during the reigns of her predecessors: her brother, Edward VI (1547–1553), and her

In 1555 bishops Hugh Latimer and Nicholas Ridley are burned at the stake for their Protestant beliefs.

father, Henry VIII (1509–1547). Determined to return England to what she considered to be the one true faith—Roman Catholicism—Mary sincerely believed that God wanted her to stamp out Protestantism by whatever means necessary.

During Mary's reign, all convicted heretics were given the opportunity to recant: to renounce their unorthodox beliefs and rejoin the Catholic Church. Mary, however, felt that she had no choice but to destroy those Protestants like Latimer and Ridley who stubbornly refused to admit the error of their ways. Traditionally, a monarch was held responsible for the spiritual health of his or her subjects, and Mary never doubted for a moment that Catholicism was the sole means of salvation for her people as well as herself. It was her sacred duty to silence the Protestants, she believed, for the heretics not only endangered their own immortal souls but also corrupted others by their wicked teachings and example. To her dying day, Mary remained convinced of the justice of the bloody executions for which she earned her macabre nickname.

Mary's absolute conviction that her way to God was the only one was an attitude shared by many of her contemporaries. Religious oppression and violence were rampant on the European continent during the sixteenth century, and thousands were slaughtered in Spain, the Netherlands, France, and what is today Germany because of their spiritual opinions. Yet if the number of dissenters killed under Mary's rule appears modest compared to the thousands—Protestant and Catholic alike—who died for their beliefs in Europe, the scale of Mary's persecutions was far greater than anything England had ever before experienced. Even in an age accustomed to brutal punishments and frequent state executions, the burning of nearly three hundred Protestant men and women horrified and repulsed Mary's subjects, including many who shared the queen's Catholic faith. Nearly five hundred years after her death, Mary is still remembered in the country that she sought to reclaim for Catholic Christianity not as a redeemer but as Bloody Mary, the ruthless murderer of innocent martyrs.

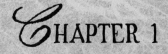

CHAPTER 1

THE YOUNG PRINCESS

$\mathcal{S}$hortly before dawn on February 18, 1516, a child was born to King Henry VIII and his wife, Catherine of Aragon. During the seven years since their wedding, the twenty-four-year-old English monarch and his thirty-year-old queen had endured three miscarriages and the deaths of two infant sons. Consequently, the birth of a healthy baby to the royal couple in the winter of 1516 sparked celebrations throughout the realm. Yet the celebrating, although heartfelt, was restrained

King Henry VIII is depicted as an imposing monarch in this portrait from the 1530s.

because the child, soon to be christened Mary, was not the male heir Henry Tudor and his subjects had long hoped for.

A Female Heir

Henry's deep-seated desire for a son was rooted in ancient tradition. In England and throughout Europe, it was taken for granted that one of a king's most important duties was to produce a male heir. As of the early sixteenth century, only a handful of European queens had ever governed in their own right, and just one woman, Henry I's daughter, Matilda, had ever ruled England. Matilda's reign in the early 1200s ended almost before it began, however, when the English nobility overthrew the new queen in favor of her male cousin, Stephen of Blois.

Women were unfit to rule, it was popularly believed, because they were inferior to men, both in intellect and character. The "weaker sex" supposedly possessed neither the wisdom nor the moral strength required to lead effectively. A female's proper place was not in the public sphere, most people agreed, but in the home with her husband and children.

Moreover, it was reasoned that because a wife was obliged by law to hand over all her property to her husband and obey him in all things, a married female ruler could place her realm in a highly vulnerable position. This was a critical point as all monarchs, male and female, were expected to wed in order to produce heirs and guarantee the succession. A queen was counted on to marry royalty— to wed anyone less exalted would be an insult to her country. More often than not, this meant she must find a spouse outside her own kingdom, a foreigner who might attempt to bend his

The deeply religious Catherine of Aragon was briefly married to Arthur Tudor, Henry's older brother.

wife—and her realm—to his own will. Consequently, Henry and his subjects worried that a female successor might place the very independence of their nation in jeopardy.

A Royal Pawn

In 1516 Henry, although obviously disappointed by Mary's gender, remained optimistic regarding a male

King Henry VII (pictured) arranged the marriage of Catherine to Henry VIII.

heir. "The queen and I are both young," he told the Venetian diplomat Giusinian shortly after Mary's birth, "and if it is a girl this time, by God's grace the boys will follow."[3] Meanwhile, Henry took comfort in the knowledge that a princess could be a useful diplomatic tool. In sixteenth-century Europe, rulers routinely arranged marriages between their daughters and foreign royalty for political, trade, and military advantages. Treated as little more than pawns on a marital chessboard, princesses often found themselves betrothed (promised in marriage) at an early age to complete strangers. Mary's own mother, Catherine of Aragon, had been promised by her father, King Ferdinand, to Arthur Tudor, Henry VII's oldest son and heir, when she was still a girl. In 1501 the sixteen-year-old Spanish princess set sail for England to meet—and wed—her fifteen-year-old fiancé. Within five months of the wedding, Arthur was dead, probably from tuberculosis. Almost immediately, Ferdinand began negotiations with Henry VII for a new contract to unite Catherine with the English monarch's second son, the future King Henry VIII.

Like his father-in-law, King Ferdinand, Henry Tudor was eager to make the most of his daughter's diplomatic value. When Mary was just two years old, he arranged for her to wed the dauphin, the infant heir of the French king, Francis I. Henry viewed the engagement as an opportunity to cement a treaty of friendship with one of England's chief rivals. In September 1518 a solemn betrothal ceremony was held at Greenwich Palace near London to seal the alliance between Francis and Henry. Little Mary, her gold-red curls tucked beneath a jewel-studded cap, listened quietly in her nurse's arms as her parents consented to the marriage on her behalf and a French envoy consented for the dauphin. The actual wedding was to be postponed for more than a decade until the dauphin turned fourteen, the traditional minimum age of marriage for a male. Still confident that Catherine would provide him with a male heir, Henry did not appear at all worried that his French son-in-law might ascend the English throne after his death.

By Mary's sixth birthday, her father had discarded the French match in favor of an even more advantageous alliance. Mary's new fiancé was her twenty-two-year-old cousin, Charles V, the mightiest ruler in Europe. As both king of Spain and Holy Roman Emperor, Charles held sway over much of western Europe, including most of modern-day Spain, Germany, Austria, the Netherlands, Belgium, and portions of Italy. The emperor immediately agreed to Henry's request to delay the wedding until Mary turned twelve but accepted his dowry offer of eighty thousand pounds with great reluctance. (In Mary's time, brides from royal or aristocratic families were expected to bring dowries, or bridal gifts, to their grooms in the form of money, land, or goods.) Although disappointed by the size of Mary's

While still a child, Princess Mary was betrothed to Charles V, the king of Spain and Holy Roman Emperor.

dowry, Charles nonetheless saw the marriage compact as an excellent opportunity to cement an alliance with England against Spain's archenemy, France.

The Education of a Princess

It is doubtful that young Mary gave much thought to her new fiancé in far-off Spain. Once she turned seven and her formal schooling began, most of the princess's waking hours were devoted to her lessons.

Catherine, who spoke several languages and was unusually well read for a woman of her era, was determined to give her daughter a superior education. At the queen's request, the Spanish scholar Luis Vives designed a curriculum for Mary centered on the classic writings of ancient Greece and Rome, which she was to study in their original Greek and Latin. The young princess picked up new languages—both ancient and modern—with ease. By age ten, she could translate almost any passage from Latin into English and was proficient in Greek, French, Spanish, and Italian. Mary was also an accomplished musician who excelled at the virginal, a keyboard instrument, and the lute, a stringed instrument similar to a guitar.

Thanks to Catherine, Mary's training in classical literature and languages was extraordinarily demanding

17

for a girl of her time. Yet neither Mary's mother nor her tutors taught the princess to see herself as the intellectual or moral equal of a male, as the study program they designed for her reveals. For example, Vives forbade Mary to read popular romances on the grounds that girls were impressionable and therefore more likely to be led astray by improper books than boys were. Nor was the princess encouraged to read works on the art of governing. Political instruction was a waste of Mary's time, it was agreed, for even if she did inherit the crown, her husband and male advisers would undoubtedly direct the affairs of state.

A Lonely Childhood

There is no evidence that Mary shared her lessons with classmates or even played regularly with other children. The princess seems to have passed most of her childhood in the company of adults, particularly her governesses, tutors, and ladies-in-waiting. Two adults Mary saw relatively little of, however, were her parents.

As was customary for royal children, by the time the princess was three years old she had her own separate household, a miniature royal court complete with dozens of gentlewomen and servants, a treasurer, and a Catholic chaplain, who counseled Mary in spiritual

For health reasons, Mary spent much of her childhood moving from one manor house to another throughout the English countryside.

matters and conducted daily religious services. Mary visited her parents chiefly on holidays, particularly Christmas and Easter. During the rest of the year, she and her entourage rotated among several different manors in the English countryside. Mary lived in an era when the majority of children did not survive to adulthood and London, England's dirty and congested capital, was considered too unhealthy for the young princess. Health concerns were also at the root of Mary's regular migrations from one manor house to another. In an age before indoor plumbing, conditions in the crowded manors quickly became unsanitary.

Consequently, Mary and her large retinue remained for only a few weeks at a particular residence. After their departure, the empty house was thoroughly scrubbed and aired in preparation for the next royal visit.

The young Mary (pictured) had a close relationship with her mother, sharing her deep devotion to the Catholic faith.

Although the amount of time that she spent in the company of either of her parents was limited, Mary enjoyed an unusually close bond with Catherine, who was devoted to her only surviving child. Mother and daughter shared much in common, including a love for learning and music as well as an unwavering loyalty to their Catholic religion.

Mary's relationship with her father was more complicated. Henry VIII was clearly proud of his accomplished daughter. He especially liked to show off Mary's musical talents and frequently asked her to play a tune on the virginal for visiting noblemen or ambassadors. Yet Henry seems to have cherished the young princess more for her potential value in the royal marriage market than he did for herself. The king often referred to Mary as "the greatest pearl in the kingdom," writes historian Carolly Erickson, "a name that aptly conveyed her worth in Henry's eyes. She was a treasure to be protected, hoarded, and, when the time came, spent to procure a lasting diplomatic advantage."[4]

A New Title and a New Fiancé

In the summer of 1525, when Mary was nine, her father bestowed a lofty new title upon "the greatest pearl" in his kingdom: Princess of Wales. Mary and more than three hundred servants and aristocratic attendants were to depart immediately for Ludlow Castle on the English-Welsh border. To preside over an imposing court in her own castle was a heady experience for the little girl. Some members of Mary's entourage even wondered if her sudden rise in status meant that the king had finally reconciled himself to the idea of a female successor. Ever since Edward I conquered Wales in the 1300s, English monarchs had granted the title Prince of Wales to their eldest sons and heirs. By 1525, when Mary received the title, it had begun to look as if Catherine might never produce a healthy male heir for England. In fact, the forty-year-old queen had become pregnant only once in the nearly ten years since Mary's birth, and that baby, a girl, had been born dead.

While the new Princess of Wales held court at Ludlow, back in England Henry busily negotiated yet another match for his daughter. His treasury depleted by a series of expensive military campaigns, Charles V had jilted Mary in favor of Portugal's Princess Isabella, who came with a considerably larger dowry than Henry was prepared to offer with his daughter. With Charles out of the picture, Henry refocused his attention on the French royal family. By early 1527 he and Francis I had hammered out a new betrothal contract between Mary and the French monarch's second son, Henry.

In April Mary was ordered to leave Wales for Greenwich Palace, where her father planned to host a round of banquets and balls in honor of the new Anglo-French alliance. Mary had much to look forward to as she set off on the long journey home—at eleven, she was finally considered old enough to take part in all the grown-up festivities.

At the great celebrations held at Greenwich that May, Mary, adorned in a sumptuous assortment of new

With her new title of Princess of Wales, Mary lived here at Ludlow Castle with her entourage.

gowns and jewels, was the star attraction. Francis's
envoys sent glowing reports to the French king about
the princess in which they praised her luxuriant golden-
red curls, clear complexion, and remarkable aptitude for
languages. The ambassadors had just one reservation
about Francis's future daughter-in-law. Mary, they
noted, was small and underdeveloped for her age.
Consequently, although she was nearly twelve—the
minimum legal age of marriage for a girl—the envoys
thought that she would not be ready to wed until after
her fourteenth birthday.

Henry became infatuated with Anne Boleyn, shown here, and began to think of ways to end his marriage to Catherine.

"The King's Great Matter"

A few weeks after the betrothal festivities, a disturbing rumor began to spread through Henry's court: Bitterly disappointed by his wife's failure to produce a son, the king wanted to annul (cancel) his marriage to Catherine. Henry already had a new queen in mind, it was said, a spirited and attractive lady-in-waiting by the name of Anne Boleyn. People could not help but note that Boleyn was only in her early twenties and had many years of childbearing ahead of her.

Henry's alleged campaign to rid himself of his middle-aged wife in order to replace her with the youthful Boleyn soon came to be known around court as "the king's great matter."

By the summer of 1527 it had become evident that the rumors were true. That July Henry informed Catherine that he considered their marriage unlawful and had applied to Pope Clement VII in Rome for an annulment. As the head of the Catholic Church, Clement alone had the authority to declare the king and queen's marriage null and void. Certain that he had strong religious grounds for the annulment, Henry was optimistic that the pope would honor his request. His union with Arthur's widow in 1509 had violated biblical law because the book of Leviticus in the Old Testament specifically prohibited marriage between a man and his brother's wife, Henry argued. Catherine's failure to give him a healthy son after nearly two decades of marriage, he reasoned, was God's punishment for their sinful relationship.

Henry quickly discovered, however, that one crucial obstacle stood between him and the

For political reasons, Pope Clement VII was hesitant to annul Henry's marriage to Catherine.

dissolution of his marriage: his wife. Convinced that God had sanctioned her union with Henry, Catherine was utterly opposed to the annulment. Her conscience was clear, she told the king. Pope Julius II had given them special permission to marry in 1509, Catherine reminded Henry, after she swore that her marriage with his ailing older brother had never been consummated and that she was still a virgin.

Under other circumstances, Catherine's opposition to the annulment probably would not have posed a problem for Henry. Popes generally accommodated kings in such matters, and many a ruler had been granted an annulment from a barren or unwanted wife despite her objections. The queen of England, however, was a special case, for she had the backing of the one ruler Clement feared even more than the strong-willed Henry: Catherine's nephew, Charles V. The Holy Roman Emperor's forces controlled large portions of Italy, and a mutinous imperial army had recently looted Rome and even held the pope hostage for a time. Consequently, Clement was hesitant to cross Charles, who considered Henry's callous treatment of his aunt as an insult to his entire family. Reluctant to commit himself one way or the other, the pope dragged his feet regarding Henry's request; by 1631, four years after the king first applied to Rome for an annulment, Clement had still failed to make a ruling.

A Shattered Family

It is impossible to say when Mary first became aware of her parents' marital troubles. The princess maintained her own household throughout her early teens and spent most of her time in the English countryside at one royal manor or another. On those occasions when she visited Henry's court, however, she would certainly have heard rumors of her parents' dispute, especially as the stalemate between the king and the pope dragged on month after frustrating month.

As the pope dithered regarding the annulment, to the dismay of the royal family Henry became ever more open in his affection for Anne Boleyn and his disdain for the wife who refused to release him. Brokenhearted and humiliated, the queen took what solace she could in her religion and her beloved daughter. As she is barely mentioned in the surviving letters or official records of the period, historians know little about Mary's life during this trying time. "One thing is very clear, however," writes Carolly Erickson, "Mary watched and wept over her mother's trials, and took her part."[5] In light of Mary's close relationship with her mother, it was hardly surprising that she should have taken Catherine's side in the conflict. Yet Mary must also have realized that her own cause and that of her mother were inextricably intertwined. If the pope declared her parents' marriage null and void, Mary automatically became illegitimate. Both her title and her marital prospects would be jeopardized. Indeed, by 1530, the year that Mary turned fourteen and should have wed Prince Henry, Francis I had already backed out of the contract that bound his son to Henry's daughter, a young woman whose status and prospects appeared more uncertain with each passing year.

Catherine stands before officials ruling on the legitimacy of her marriage to King Henry, who sits in the background.

In July 1531 any hopes that Mary may have cherished for reconciliation between her parents were shattered when Henry finally ordered Catherine to leave his court for good. Soon after, in a fit of pique, he forbade his obstinate queen to ever see her daughter again. Mary was devastated. Her mother, the person to whom she had always been the closest, was to be taken from her forever. Just as Catherine had always done in times of crisis, Mary now turned for comfort and strength to what had been the one constant in her young life aside from her mother's love: her Catholic faith.

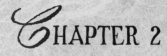

CHAPTER 2

"THE MOST UNHAPPY LADY IN CHRISTENDOM"

In February 1533, unwilling to wait any longer for Pope Clement to rule on the annulment of his marriage to Mary's mother, Henry VIII took matters into his own hands. On his insistence, Parliament, England's national legislative body, decreed that all legal matters, spiritual as well as worldly, would henceforth be decided in England. Now the pope and his colleagues in Rome no longer possessed the authority to pass judgment on Henry's marriage to Catherine. Henry then commanded his loyal supporter, Thomas Cranmer, the newly appointed archbishop of Canterbury and England's highest-ranking church official, to review his annulment petition. In May Cranmer obligingly pronounced the king and queen's union illegal on the grounds that Catherine was the widow of Henry's brother.

Henry, however, had not waited for the official dissolution of his marriage to Catherine before he took a new bride. In January 1533 he secretly wed Anne Boleyn after she informed him that she was pregnant with his child. On June 1, barely more than a week after he annulled Henry and Catherine's marriage, Cranmer crowned an obviously expectant Anne as England's new queen.

As the Archbishop of Canterbury, Thomas Cranmer annulled the marriage of Catherine and Henry in 1533.

Mary's status and role in the royal court were now more uncertain than ever before. By ruling that her parents' marriage had never been valid, Cranmer had made the seventeen-year-old princess illegitimate by the laws of England. According to long-standing tradition, a king's illegitimate children were not deemed suitable heirs to the throne. Confident that Anne would soon provide him with the much-desired male successor, Henry hardened his heart against his hurt and indignant daughter. Already forbidden to see Catherine, Mary was told that she could no longer even exchange letters with her mother.

Henry courts Anne Boleyn, in this painting. In 1533 Henry and Anne wed.

Princess Elizabeth and Lady Mary

Three months after her coronation on September 7, 1533, Anne gave birth to a healthy baby at Greenwich Palace. To Henry's immense frustration, the child was a girl, soon to be named Elizabeth. Despite his disappointment, the king, resolved to put a good face on the birth before the world, immediately pronounced the infant the new Princess of Wales. Soon after, an official written order was delivered to

Mary at the country estate where she then resided. Addressed to "the Lady Mary, the King's daughter,"[6] the letter informed Mary that she could no longer refer to herself as the Princess of Wales.

Mary was outraged. Just as her mother had refused to go along with Henry's annulment scheme, Mary was determined to resist her father's efforts to rob her of what she viewed as her rightful title. In her terse reply to Henry, Mary stubbornly insisted that she was the king's lawful child, "born in true matrimony," and signed herself, "your humble daughter, Mary, *Princess.*"[7]

Mary's punishment for her disobedience to the crown was swift and humiliating. She was stripped of her personal entourage and income and ordered to join Elizabeth's household as one of the infant princess's ladies-in-waiting. Cut off from her old friends and supporters, Mary was forced to tag along with the little girl and her attendants as they moved from one country manor to another. Whenever Elizabeth visited the royal court, however, her older sister stayed behind: The king and queen had made it clear that they wanted nothing to do with Mary until she agreed to acknowledge her own illegitimacy and the lawfulness of Henry's new marriage.

Mary's obstinate defiance seems to have angered Anne even more than it did Henry. Every bit as strong-willed and proud as her stepdaughter, Anne resented Mary's haughty refusal to recognize her as the rightful queen. The former princess's popularity among the common folk, who generally sympathized with Mary's plight, further annoyed Anne. Reports had reached the queen that people ran out of their houses and fields to greet Mary as she passed by on her way from one country residence to another. In some villages that Mary traveled through, Anne complained bitterly, "As much rejoicing went on as if God Almighty had come down from heaven."[8]

The new queen took every opportunity to put Henry's uppity daughter in her place. Anne commanded Lady Shelton, her aunt and the mistress of young Elizabeth's household, to slap and curse at the girl whenever she referred to herself as Princess Mary instead of Lady Mary. When Mary dared to complain to the king about her demeaning treatment, Anne angrily confiscated all of her jewelry and her best gowns. According to Eustace Chapuys, Charles V's ambassador and Mary's loyal friend, at one point the queen even threatened to have her troublesome stepdaughter poisoned.

Mary's Physical and Spiritual Trials

Bored, lonely, and often frightened for her own safety, Mary endured two long years in her half sister's household. Mary's physical and psychological health both suffered under the strain of her forced confinement. From 1534 to 1536, the regular dispatches that Chapuys sent to Charles regarding the former princess were filled with accounts of her persistent headaches, stomach and menstrual ailments, heart palpitations, insomnia, and depression.

A series of shocking political and religious developments only added to Mary's distress during these years. In March 1534, a few months after Mary joined Elizabeth's household, Pope Clement finally announced his verdict regarding her parents' marriage. Catherine and Henry's union of 1509 was legal and binding, the pope declared, and Henry must either renounce his marriage with Anne at once or face expulsion from the Roman Catholic Church. Soon after the pope's pronouncement, a defiant Henry pushed legislation through Parliament that settled the English succession in his children by Anne Boleyn. In effect, the Act of Succession of 1534 confirmed Mary's illegitimate status and removal from the line of succession and made Elizabeth the heir to the throne, at least until such time as Anne produced a son.

Henry also persuaded Parliament to approve another critical piece of legislation in 1534 that appalled both

Sir Thomas More refused to acknowledge Henry as the supreme head of the new Church of England.

Mary and her fervently Catholic mother, Catherine of Aragon. According to the Act of Supremacy, the English monarch rather than the pope was now the ultimate authority on all religious matters in the kingdom. Henry's subjects were required to swear an oath that renounced the pope's authority and recognized the king as the supreme head of the newly created Church of England. Anyone who refused to take the so-called Oath of Supremacy or disputed the lawfulness of Henry and Anne's marriage would be charged with high treason and punished accordingly, the king proclaimed.

Few of Henry's subjects dared to disobey their sovereign. Those who did, including Henry's former lord chancellor (chief adviser), the distinguished writer and philosopher Sir Thomas More, were harshly punished for their defiance. During the summer of 1535 More and John Fisher, bishop of Rochester, were beheaded, and seven monks were hanged because they had refused to take the oath. Four of the condemned monks were also drawn and quartered, an unusually cruel punishment even in an era known for its brutal executions. The four men were cut down from the gallows while they were still alive, and their intestines were cut out and burned before their eyes. Finally, the monks were beheaded and their torsos were sliced into quarters.

Soon after the grisly executions, a report reached Mary that Henry had threatened to behead her and her mother unless they swore to the new Act of Succession and the Act of Supremacy. Despite the terrifying rumor, however, the king did not compel his daughter and former wife to take the oaths during the bloody summer of 1535. Whether his decision to spare the two women was motivated by genuine compassion or by practical political considerations is impossible to say. Many people in England admired Catherine and her daughter for their piety and

Refusing to take the Oath of Supremacy, John Fisher (pictured) and More were beheaded for high treason in 1535.

courage and openly sympathized with them. Consequently, Henry may have worried that in the wake of his executions of More, Fisher, and the hapless monks, Mary's and Catherine's deaths might arouse public passions to the point of a full-scale rebellion.

Two Deaths and a Marriage

In January 1536, just weeks before her twentieth birthday, Mary received devastating news: Her adored mother, whom she had not seen for nearly five years, was dead. Mary had known for some time that her mother's health was fragile, but her pleas to visit Catherine at Kimbolton Castle, where the former queen lived under virtual house arrest, had been met with stony silence from the king. Now her mother was gone, and Mary had not even had a chance to say good-bye.

On the day of Catherine's burial, the woman Mary had always considered as her mother's greatest enemy suffered a terrible loss of her own. On January 29, 1536, Anne Boleyn miscarried her second child—a boy, according to the midwives who examined the fetus. Henry was remarkably unsympathetic. Instead of comforting his anguished wife, he berated Anne for her failed pregnancy. During the three years since their wedding, the king had become increasingly dissatisfied with his

THE TOWER OF LONDON

The Tower of London, where Anne Boleyn was incarcerated and eventually executed in the spring of 1536, was not always a state prison. The first structure in what eventually became an eighteen-acre complex of more than a dozen towers and other buildings along the north bank of the Thames River was built by William, Duke of Normandy, soon after he conquered England in 1066. William intended his massive stone tower to serve as a fortress and royal arsenal. Over the next several centuries, however, the continually expanding complex along the Thames took on a number of additional functions, including serving as a royal residence, a mint, a public-records office, and a menagerie, or zoo.

By the time Henry VIII ascended the throne in the early sixteenth century, the Tower of London had also become England's chief prison and place of execution for men and women accused of treason and other political crimes. Generally, members of the nobility, and particularly noblewomen, were executed privately on the Tower Green. High-ranking criminals like Anne Boleyn were usually beheaded and then buried in the Chapel of St. Peter ad Vincula, which bordered the Tower Green. The Tower's less illustrious prisoners were most often execut-ed by hanging on the Tower Hill, which was located just outside of the complex.

An individual's social standing generally determined the conditions of his or her imprisonment in the Tower as well as his or her place and method of execution. Aristocratic prisoners were routinely allowed special privileges, such as playing cards, books, visitors, and regular walks on the walls or in the yard. On the other hand, the Tower's wealthier inhabitants were also expected to pay for their own food and other necessities. The royal government provided the lieutenant or chief officer of the Tower with a yearly allowance for feeding and clothing the fortress's poorer occupants.

This engraving shows the Tower of London as it looked in the sixteenth century.

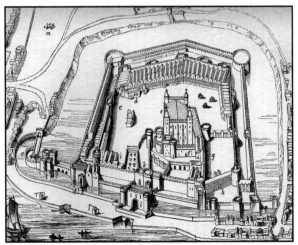

strong-minded and outspoken queen. In the wake of Anne's miscarriage, he concluded that their union had been a mistake from the beginning. God would never bless their marriage with healthy sons, he said, because Anne had used witchcraft to trick him into marrying her against his will. Moreover, Henry believed he had found the perfect replacement for his conniving second wife: a sweet-tempered and pious lady-in-waiting to the queen named Jane Seymour. The king was optimistic that

In 1536 Anne Boleyn, sitting at the head of the table, is arrested on trumped-up charges of adultery and high treason.

Seymour would bring him a son at last; not only was Seymour several years younger than Anne, but she came from a large family that included plenty of males.

Determined to rid himself of Anne Boleyn, Henry considered his options. For a time, the king toyed with the idea of asking Cranmer for another annulment. By the spring of 1536, however, he had resolved to pursue a speedier course of action. On May 2 Henry ordered the queen's arrest and imprisonment in the Tower of London on several

In May 1536, Henry took Jane Seymour as his third wife.

trumped-up charges, including adultery with her own brother. On May 19 Anne was beheaded on the Tower Green, and her remains were unceremoniously stuffed into an old arrow chest as no one had thought to prepare a proper coffin for the woman who had once been the king's great passion. Eleven days later Henry wed Jane Seymour. With both his ex-wives now dead,

41

he felt confident that no one could dispute the legality of this latest marriage or of the legitimacy of the sons he hoped his union with Seymour would soon produce.

Mary Loses Her Nerve

With her old enemy, Anne Boleyn, out of her father's life for good, Mary also felt hopeful about the future. Influenced by her mother, Mary had always faulted Anne for Henry's callous behavior toward his first wife and eldest daughter. Like Catherine, Mary believed that the former lady-in-waiting had bewitched the king and turned him against all that he had once held dear. Now that Anne could no longer work her evil spell over Henry, Mary looked forward to a swift return to her father's good graces.

Mary was in for a rude awakening. Although Henry's kindhearted new queen, Jane Seymour, urged him to call his daughter back to court immediately, the king refused to reconcile with Mary until she admitted to the unlawfulness of her parents' marriage and her own illegitimacy. In addition, Henry declared, Mary must formally deny the authority of the pope and recognize the king as the supreme head of the Church of England. Anne's death had not brought the miraculous transformation in Henry's attitude that Mary had so confidently expected; if anything, the king now seemed more determined than ever to break his eldest daughter's spirit.

In the summer of 1536, Henry placed unprecedented pressure on his rebellious firstborn when he demanded that Mary sign a formal letter of submission to him. The letter declared that Catherine and Henry's marriage was invalid, that Mary herself was illegitimate, and that the pope no longer possessed any influence over the English church. If Mary signed the document, Henry's messengers informed her, she would be assured of her father's goodwill. If she refused, they warned, she could very well find herself in the Tower of London, charged with high treason against the crown, a crime punishable by death.

Henry had launched his new campaign to bring Mary to her knees at a time when the twenty-year-old was at her most vulnerable. Still depressed by the loss of her beloved mother and plagued by chronic insomnia and headaches, Mary was pushed to the limits of her endurance by the king's bullying. Even Mary's fervent champion, Chapuys, concerned about the ex-princess's fragile mental and physical health, urged her to give in. Following yet another sleepless night, on June 22, 1536, Mary finally buckled and signed the hated concession. Convinced that she had betrayed her mother's good name and, even worse, her religious principles, Mary was immediately filled with remorse. She begged Chapuys to travel to Rome on her behalf to ask the pope for his forgiveness and understanding. Determined to ease his distraught young friend's mind, Chapuys assured Mary that the pope would surely not consider as binding a submission that had been obtained under such extreme pressure.

A Male Heir at Last

Despite Mary's deep misgivings regarding her submission to the king, in many ways her life improved after she signed the hated document. Although she did not regain her title of princess, by the autumn Mary's private household had been restored and she had become a regular visitor at Henry's court. She genuinely admired her kind and devout new stepmother, Jane, and soon considered the young queen as one of her dearest friends.

In view of the close relationship between Mary and the queen, it seemed fitting that Mary should serve as godmother to the child born to Jane and Henry on October 12, 1537. To the delight of the king and the entire English nation, the baby was a healthy boy, Prince Edward. All over the kingdom church bells pealed and people abandoned their workshops and farm fields to celebrate the wonderful news that at long last England had a male heir.

Yet joy turned to sorrow when twelve days after the prince's birth Jane Seymour died, probably as the result of a bacterial infection. Now all three of Henry's children—Mary, Elizabeth, and Edward—were motherless. Mary was devastated by the loss of her trusted friend and confidant. At just twenty-one years old, it seemed that she had already endured enough grief and disappointment to last a lifetime.

"The Most Unhappy Lady in Christendom"

Mary's anguish after the queen's death was deepened by her growing dismay regarding the state of her beloved Catholicism in England. Shortly after his marriage to Jane, Henry had launched a ruthless campaign to shut down the kingdom's monasteries and nunneries. Because their inhabitants still accepted the authority of the pope, the destruction of the religious houses was necessary to complete England's break with Rome, Henry maintained. Yet the king and his officials had another, even more pressing motive for their attack on the convents and monasteries: The government was short on money, and the religious houses possessed enormous wealth, mainly in the form of thousands of acres of fertile land. To Mary's disgust, by 1542 Henry had forced the closing of every one of the kingdom's more than five hundred religious houses and had confiscated church property worth more than £ 1 million. Most of the property was then sold or given to the king's aristocratic supporters.

Henry's appalling plunder of England's monasteries and nunneries was not the only thing that weighed on Mary's mind during the late 1530s and early 1540s. She had also become increasingly concerned about her own

Henry used his break with Rome as an excuse to confiscate church property such as this abbey in southern England.

future. Soon after Mary's submission to him in June 1537, Henry resumed his quest to secure a titled husband for his eldest daughter. The king's efforts, however, had all come to nothing. As Mary herself understood only too well, her value in the royal marriage market dropped sharply after her parents' marriage was annulled and she was officially removed from the line of succession.

By her twenty-fifth birthday, with no prince or even a high-ranking nobleman prepared to bid for her hand, Mary had come to the bitter conclusion that as long as her father continued to deny the lawfulness of his union with Catherine, marriage and motherhood would remain forever beyond her reach. With no clear role or standing in Henry's court, the former princess felt useless and insignificant; she was, she confided bitterly to a friend, "only the Lady Mary, and the most unhappy lady in Christendom."[9]

47

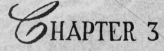

CHAPTER 3

MARY'S CHANGING FORTUNES

By her late twenties, Mary's life had changed in dramatic and unexpected ways. By the beginning of 1543, she had managed to carve out a new place for herself in Henry's court and affections following the execution of his fifth wife, Catherine Howard, for adultery. (Henry's fourth wife was the German princess Anne of Cleves, whom he met for the first time after their betrothal in 1540. He quickly decided that Anne was not to his taste and had the marriage annulled.) After Howard's disgrace and beheading, the dejected king turned to his eldest daughter for comfort and companionship. Despite their tumultuous past, Mary still yearned for her father's affection. Consequently, she willingly devoted herself to the aging king, acting as his hostess at court functions and sitting by his sickbed whenever he fell ill.

A New Stepmother and a New Act of Succession

In July 1543 Henry Tudor married his sixth and last wife, a gentle and pious widow named Catherine Parr. At thirty-one, Catherine was just four years older than Mary, and the two women became fast friends. Like Mary and her mother, the first Queen Catherine, Mary and Catherine Parr had much in common, including a love for books and learning, as well as a deep devotion to their Christian faith.

The kindhearted new queen encouraged Henry to develop a closer relationship with all three of his children. Thanks to Catherine's influence, in 1544 Henry restored both Mary and eleven-year-old Elizabeth to the line of

In 1542 Henry executed Catherine Howard, his fifth wife, for adultery.

Henry's sixth and last wife, Catherine Parr, encouraged the king to improve his relationship with his daughters and son.

succession. According to the Act of Succession approved by Parliament that year, in the event that Edward died without children, Mary became queen. Elizabeth stood next in line to inherit the crown after Mary and any children she might have. Although Mary was gratified to be back in the succession, to her dismay the act did nothing to remove the shadow of illegitimacy that had hung over her for the last decade. Nor did it legitimize her half sister, Elizabeth, whose parents' marriage had been annulled by royal decree soon after Anne Boleyn's execution.

During the two years following the passage of the new Act of Succession, Henry's health steadily deteriorated. On the morning of January 28, 1547, the fifty-six-year-old king breathed for the last time. In the will he had composed shortly before his death, Henry confirmed his choice of Mary as Edward's successor should Edward die childless. In addition, the will called for a sixteen-man council to advise Edward until he reached the age of eighteen. Until the king was old enough to rule independently, the council was also given the authority to approve Mary's and Elizabeth's choice of husband. If they wed without the council's approval, Henry's daughters were to be removed from the line of succession.

The Boy King

On February 20, 1547, the nine-year-old heir to the English throne was crowned King Edward VI in a magnificent ceremony at Westminster Abbey in London. To Mary's disappointment, she was not invited to witness the proceedings. Despite the more than twenty-year difference in their ages, Mary and the new king had always been close. From the start, Edward had treated Mary more like a mother than a sibling. He often asked for Mary's advice, and when she was sick with one of her frequent headaches or digestive ailments, he wrote her long, affectionate notes. After Edward was crowned, however, brother and sister drifted ever farther apart.

As soon as Edward ascended the throne, he found himself under the strict supervision of the council and

51

particularly its leader, his uncle, Edward Seymour, the Duke of Somerset. As lord protector of the new king, Somerset was resolved to shield Edward from any harmful influences, which to the duke's way of thinking most definitely included Mary Tudor.

To Somerset and his fellow councilors, Mary represented a potentially serious challenge to their control over the king. At the heart of their concerns was Mary's well-known loyalty to traditional Catholic practices and teachings. The lord protector and his council were followers of the new Protestant faith that had first developed in western Europe three decades earlier. Determined to bring the new king up as a Protestant, they hoped to limit Edward's contact with his ardently Catholic eldest sister as much as possible.

The Development of Protestantism

Protestant Christianity has its roots in the Reformation, the great religious movement that swept through western Europe during the sixteenth century. Most historians date the beginning of the Reformation to 1517, the year that the German monk Martin Luther nailed his famous Ninety-five Theses (arguments) to the door of the Castle Church in Wittenburg. In his theses, Luther blasted local clergymen who sold indulgences (pardons for sins) to

HENRY VIII's FIFTH WIFE: CATHERINE HOWARD

Vivacious Catherine Howard was only nineteen years old when she married Henry VIII on July 28, 1540, just two weeks after the forty-nine-year-old king's annulment from the German princess Anne of Cleves. A member of one of England's oldest and most illustrious families, Catherine was the daughter of Lord Edmund Howard and the niece of Thomas Howard, the powerful Duke of

Many historians believe that Catherine Howard actually was unfaithful to Henry.

Norfolk. She was also the cousin of Henry's second wife, Anne Boleyn, a relationship that inevitably put a barrier between the new queen and her stepdaughter, Lady Mary.

Although Henry was clearly infatuated with his attractive teenage bride, his fifth marriage was destined to be short-lived. A little more than a year after the wedding, reports surfaced at court that Catherine had had a lover before her betrothal to Henry. At first, Henry was inclined to forgive the queen for her youthful indiscretion. The king's attitude toward his wife changed dramatically, however, after his advisers produced convincing evidence that Catherine had also carried on an affair after her marriage. Henry was devastated by this revelation of his adored wife's infidelity; it was said that his distress was so great that he could hardly speak. According to the laws of England, a queen who committed adultery was guilty of high treason, a crime punishable by death. On February 13, 1542, therefore, twenty-one-year-old Catherine was beheaded on the Tower Green, the same spot where Anne Boleyn had met her end just six years earlier. Most historians believe that unlike her cousin Anne, however, Catherine Howard probably had actually been unfaithful to Henry.

raise money for the church and called on the pope and the rest of the Catholic leadership to renounce what he viewed as a fundamentally un-Christian practice. Sinners were saved by their faith in Jesus Christ alone, Luther insisted, and not because they donated money to the church or performed other good deeds.

Luther's criticism of church teachings and practices struck a responsive chord with many of his contemporaries. The Roman Catholic Church had monopolized religious life in Europe for hundreds of years and, like Luther, many Europeans worried that the church had become too powerful and wealthy for its own good. At the same time, they were also drawn to Luther's emphasis on salvation by faith alone and the ability of every believer to interpret the Bible for himself or herself, without the guidance of priests. The reform movement that Luther sparked in Wittenburg spread rapidly to the rest of western Europe, where it attracted particularly large followings in the Netherlands and Switzerland. At first the reformers, or Protestants, as they came to be known, tried to change the Catholic Church from within. Soon, however, they decided that the gap between their beliefs and Catholicism was too great, and they decided to forsake the old religion altogether and found their own denominations and sects.

Henry VIII had been king for a little less than a decade when Luther pinned his Ninety-five Theses to the church door at Wittenburg. When news of the rebel monk and his newfangled religious ideas reached England, Henry was appalled. Resolved to uphold the old beliefs, the king wrote a book that blasted Luther and his followers as misguided and ignorant. In gratitude, Pope Leo X awarded Henry with the title "Defender of the Faith" in 1521. Even after Henry broke with Rome and declared himself supreme head of the Church of England twelve years later, he continued to reject Protestant teachings. Henry created a separate English church in 1534 not from any desire to abandon Catholic practices and beliefs but merely to prevent the pope from any further meddling in his or his kingdom's affairs.

Mary and the New Protestant Order in England

As long as Henry lived, his religious views held sway in England. Immediately upon the king's death, however, Somerset and his council launched a determined crusade to transform England into a Protestant state. Young Edward was provided with staunchly Protestant tutors, and Thomas Cranmer was ordered to create a new

In 1517 Martin Luther posts his Ninety-five Theses on the Castle Church in Wittenburg, an act that launched the Protestant Reformation.

English prayer book and a simpler, Protestant-style communion service to replace the Catholic mass.

By 1549 the archbishop had completed his assignment. Cranmer's Book of Common Prayer laid out the order for the Church of England's new, streamlined communion service. All rites were to be conducted in English rather than the traditional Latin of the Roman Catholic mass. This change in language reflected the Protestant belief that all Christians, and not just an educated minority, should be able to understand church proceedings. To ensure that every church in England used the Book of Common Prayer, Parliament passed an oppressive new law. According to the Act of Uniformity, any clergyman who refused to adopt the new prayer book and communion rites would be fined. If the priest continued in his disobedience, he could be charged with treason and imprisoned for life.

As the Duke of Somerset and his fellow councilors might have predicted, Mary adamantly refused to have anything to do with the new prayer book and communion service. Keenly aware that the councilors frowned on her devotion to the old religion, Mary had visited the royal court only a few times since her father's death, despite her affection for her younger brother. After Parliament approved the Act of Uniformity in April 1549, she became more determined than ever to keep her distance from the boy king and his Protestant advisers. Mary had inherited four country estates from her late father, and she divided her time among them. Accompanied by her servants and aristocratic attendants, she continued to hold Latin mass in her private chapels in defiance of the new law. Mary apparently believed that as long as she remained in the countryside, far from London and the royal court, Somerset and his cronies would be content to let her go her own way.

Mary was in for a bitter surprise. In June the council officially ordered her to comply with the Act of Uniformity at once. Mary's faith had long been her chief solace and strength. Now, the government expected her to give up the traditional rites she had cherished all her life. In desperation, Mary appealed to the most powerful Catholic ruler in Europe: her cousin, the Holy Roman Emperor. Outraged by what he considered to be the council's disrespectful treatment of his relative, Charles V sent a stern letter to Somerset. Lady Mary must be allowed to practice her faith, he informed the lord protector, without any governmental interference.

Loath to cross the powerful emperor Charles, Somerset reluctantly backed down. Among Mary's personal entourage were four Catholic chaplains. These four priests, the duke promised, could still celebrate the

Completed in 1549, Thomas Cranmer's Book of Common Prayer brought change to the Church of England.

Latin mass in the privacy of Mary's own chapels. Despite Charles's repeated demands, however, Somerset refused to put his promise to Mary in writing. Both Mary and the emperor would have to be satisfied with a verbal pledge, he insisted.

Edward Versus Mary

In October 1549 Somerset, the most influential man in England since Henry VIII's death, was ousted as head of the council by one of his fellow advisers. Somerset's replacement as chief

The ambitious John Dudley (pictured) replaced Edward Seymour, the Duke of Somerset, in 1549 as effective ruler of the English realm.

guardian of young Edward VI and effective ruler of the English realm was the ruthlessly ambitious John Dudley, soon to be proclaimed the Duke of Northumberland. Dudley's rise to power had important consequences for Mary, for the council's new leader was an even more committed—and intolerant—follower of Protestantism than his predecessor had been.

Grimly determined to make Mary comply with the Act of Uniformity, unlike Somerset, the Duke of

Raised as a staunch Protestant, Edward became king in 1547 at the age of nine.

Northumberland was not about to let himself be intimidated by Charles V. Because she stood next in line to the throne, Mary's religious attitudes and actions possessed enormous political significance, Dudley believed. He worried that many of Edward's subjects secretly agreed with Mary regarding the new forms of worship and had gone along with the recent religious reforms solely to avoid punishment. Consequently, as long as Mary clung to the old faith, Northumberland feared, she had the potential to become a powerful symbol of resistance to the Protestant government. Convinced that he had little choice but to force Mary's submission, the duke sent her one hectoring letter after another in which he admonished her to give up her unlawful religious practices immediately.

By 1551 Edward himself had joined in Northumberland's crusade against the rebellious Lady

Mary. That January the thirteen-year-old king added his own postscript to one of the duke's badgering letters to his sister:

> It is a scandalous thing that so high a personage should deny our sovereignty. . . . Your nearness to us in blood, your greatness in estate, the condition of this time, maketh your fault the greater. . . . Truly sister, I will not say more and worse things, because my duty would compel me to use harsher and angrier words. But this I will say with certain intention, that I will see my laws strictly obeyed, and those who break them shall be watched and denounced.[10]

Edward's stinging rebuke devastated Mary. "Until now," writes historian Alison Plowden, "Mary had been able perhaps to comfort herself with the belief that her little brother was only a helpless tool in the hands of men like John Dudley and his cronies—that it was they, not he, who were her enemies."[11] Despite the imperious tone of Edward's letter, however, Mary clung to the hope that all was not yet lost. In the spring of 1551 she traveled to London to plead her case in person before her younger brother. Mary begged the king to let her worship as she saw fit, at least until he was old enough to rule independently. At thirteen, she insisted, Edward was simply too young to judge for himself in religious matters.

Far from being swayed by Mary's argument, the king was incensed. Mary too might have a thing or two to learn about religion, he snapped. Edward then cautioned his sister that if he failed to see a change in her behavior soon, "I could not bear it." Undeterred by the warning, Mary boldly replied that "her soul was God's and her faith she would not change."[12]

By August 1551 Edward had decided that if Mary could not be persuaded to see the error of her ways, then she must be barred from practicing the old rites altogether, even in the privacy of her own chapels. Henceforth, if her chaplains used any prayer book but the one authorized by the Act of Uniformity, Mary was informed, the disobedient priests would be arrested and imprisoned. In response, Mary sadly dismissed all but one of her chaplains and informed her servants and attendants that they could no longer attend Catholic services in her houses. Mary did not cave in to her persecutors completely, however. Each day, behind the locked doors of her private chambers, Mary's sole remaining chaplain quietly celebrated the ancient mass before a congregation of one: the Protestant king's eldest sister and presumed successor.

A Protestant Successor to Edward

That both the Act of Succession of 1544 and Henry VIII's will named the Catholic Mary as Edward's successor should the king die childless had long worried Northumberland. In early 1553 the duke's concerns regarding the succession took on a new sense of urgency when fifteen-year-old Edward developed a recurring fever and hacking cough. The young king had begun to show the signs of an advanced case of tuberculosis, the same disease that had killed his uncle, Henry VIII's brother, Arthur, fifty years earlier. Although Mary had outwardly complied with the Act of Uniformity ever since the summer of 1551, Northumberland was convinced that her Catholic loyalties were as strong as ever. If Edward succumbed to his illness, the duke feared, Mary would immediately reinstate Catholicism as England's national religion and dismiss him and every other Protestant official in the realm.

As Edward's condition worsened during the spring of 1553, Northumberland devised a desperate plan to keep Mary off the throne and maintain his own political power. At the center of Northumberland's scheme was a pious and studious teenage girl: Lady Jane Grey, the daughter of the Duke of Suffolk. As the granddaughter of Henry VIII's younger sister, fifteen-year-old Jane

63

stood next in line to the English throne after Mary and Elizabeth. In May Northumberland arranged a marriage between Jane and his own son, seventeen-year-old Guildford Dudley. Shortly after the wedding, the duke began to quietly amass weapons, provisions, and money. Now all that was left was to convince Edward to designate Jane as his successor.

Persuading Edward to leave his throne to his cousin proved an easy task for the duke. Jane was a zealous Protestant, and under the guidance of Northumberland and Cranmer, Edward had become convinced that Protestant Christianity was the sole path to salvation not only for himself but also for his subjects. Although Elizabeth, unlike her older sister Mary, was Protestant, Edward believed that she lacked Jane's religious fervor. Another point in Jane's favor was that she was already married to an Englishman from a staunchly Protestant family whereas Elizabeth was single. As queen, Edward worried, Elizabeth might wed a Catholic foreigner who would pressure her to reinstate the old religion in England. In June 1553, therefore, in direct opposition to the Act of Succession of 1544 and his father's will, Edward disinherited both Mary and Elizabeth and named Jane Grey Dudley as his successor. Now the young king could die in peace, content in the knowledge that he had guaranteed the survival of what he viewed as the one genuine religion in his realm. In accordance with Northumberland's advice, Edward did not inform Mary of this newest change in her standing and fortunes.

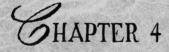

CHAPTER 4

THE NEW QUEEN

$\mathcal{O}$n July 4, 1553, Mary received an urgent message from Northumberland at her estate in Hertfordshire. The duke wanted her to leave immediately for Greenwich Palace. Mary, who had known for months that the king was ill, concluded that the summons could mean only one thing: Her fifteen-year-old brother was near death.

As she mulled over the duke's request, Mary was torn between loyalty to her brother and anxiety for herself. She knew that Edward's advisers dreaded the idea of a Catholic monarch. Perhaps they hoped to lure her to Greenwich in order to imprison or even murder her before the king died and she could claim the throne. In the end, however, Mary's strong sense of duty overcame her fears.

Despite her good intentions, Mary never made it to her brother's sickbed. On the night of July 6, a sympathizer intercepted her on the London road. The king had just passed away, he informed Mary, and she was headed straight into a trap. Mary acted quickly. Accompanied by a handful of trusted attendants, she turned around and galloped northward toward Kenninghall, her manor in Norfolk, where she had many friends among the local gentry. Mary was afraid, but she was also determined. Once she received confirmation of Edward's death, she meant to proclaim herself queen. Possession of the crown was not only her birthright, Mary believed, but also her one chance to make England Catholic again.

Queen Jane

As Mary raced toward Norfolk, back in London Northumberland was determined to keep the king's death a secret until Henry's eldest daughter could be found and arrested. Before he made his next move, Northumberland wanted the chief rival to the woman whom he hoped to install as his puppet queen safely

The dukes of Northumberland and Suffolk beg Lady Jane Grey to accept the crown of England after Edward's death in 1553.

under his control. By July 9, however, with Mary still at large, the duke decided that he could wait no longer to launch his plan to save English Protestantism and his own power. That afternoon he summoned Jane Grey Dudley to his mansion on the Thames River.

Flanked by Jane's parents and his fellow councilors, Northumberland informed his daughter-in-law that Edward was dead and she was the ruler of England. Jane, who had been kept in the dark regarding her late cousin's will, was stunned. Mary was the rightful heir, Jane tearfully insisted, and she neither wanted nor deserved the crown. In the face of relentless pressure from the council and her parents, however, the frightened teenager's resistance soon crumbled. As she reluctantly accepted the awesome responsibility her elders had thrust upon her, Jane beseeched God for his guidance. "If what hath been given to me is lawfully mine," she prayed, "may Thy Divine Majesty grant me such spirit and grace that I may govern to Thy glory and service."[13]

The next day Jane traveled by royal barge up the Thames to the capital, where she was formally proclaimed queen. Londoners greeted the news of the fifteen-year-old's ascension with dazed silence. It seemed that Jane's subjects were as dismayed about the unexpected turn of events as she was herself.

Mary Stands Her Ground

A few hours after Jane's proclamation, the council received a stern letter from Edward's original successor. Mary scolded the councilors for failing to notify her of "such a weighty matter"[14] as the king's death and commanded them to declare her queen at once. At first Northumberland and his cohorts were taken aback by Mary's haughty defiance. Yet they soon agreed that there was no genuine cause for alarm; after all, they controlled the royal treasury, the navy, and the Tower of London, the kingdom's greatest arsenal.

Mary's position, however, was stronger than the councilors could have realized. On the same day that she wrote to the council, Mary sent out dozens of letters to towns and cities throughout the realm. In the letters, she reminded her compatriots that both Henry VIII and Parliament had named her as Edward's successor and requested their assistance in her quest to secure what was rightfully hers. The response to Mary Tudor's plea for help was swift and enthusiastic. Provisions, ammunition, and men flooded into Kenninghall. By July 12 Mary had decided to leave Kenninghall for larger Framlingham Castle in Suffolk. Within a matter of days, a force of some fifteen thousand supporters, commoners and

Queen Mary imprisoned the young Jane Grey in the Tower of London, assuring her that she would not be executed.

aristocrats alike, had assembled on the castle grounds. Clearly, the majority of the English people viewed Henry Tudor's eldest surviving child as Edward's lawful successor.

Reports of Mary's growing army of sympathizers deeply alarmed the council. Northumberland was recruited to lead an army to Framlingham to crush the rebels and arrest Mary. No sooner had the duke left, however, than the crews of the royal warships mutinied and declared their allegiance to Mary. This was the final straw for the panicky councilors. On July 19 they abandoned the duke and his puppet queen and declared their support for Henry VIII's daughter. Jane was thrown into the Tower of London, and a large force was dispatched from London to arrest Northumberland, who surrendered without a fight.

A Popular and Merciful Queen

Late on the afternoon of the nineteenth, the lord mayor of London proclaimed Mary Tudor Queen Mary I in the churchyard of St. Paul's Cathedral. The city's ecstatic response to the mayor's announcement stood in stark contrast to the cool silence with which it had greeted Jane's proclamation nine days earlier. "The bonfires were without number," reported one witness, "and what with shouting and crying of the people, and ringing of the bells, there could no one hear almost what another said, besides banquetings and singing in the streets for joy."[15] Two weeks later Mary triumphantly entered the capital accompanied by thousands of well-wishers.

The extraordinary compassion shown by the queen to her enemies only added to her popularity. Just three of the conspirators—Northumberland and two of his closest collaborators—were executed. Mary pardoned most of the councilors who had backed Jane, including Jane's father, the Duke of Suffolk. She even was gracious enough to forgive the young woman who had worn her crown for nine days. Although Jane and her husband were charged with treason and imprisoned in the Tower of London Mary assured her cousin that she had no plans to execute either her or Guildford Dudley and even promised to release them as soon as it seemed prudent to do so.

Mary's remarkable generosity, even toward her would-be usurper, dismayed the advisers whom the new queen trusted and relied on above all others: Emperor Charles V; Charles's ambassador to England, Simon Renard; and her chancellor, Bishop Stephen Gardiner. All three had urged Mary to be lenient with her

Preparing to battle Northumberland's troops in 1553, Mary assembled an army of fifteen thousand men at Framlingham Castle.

opponents in order to promote peace within the realm. Yet there must be limits to the queen's mercy, they contended, and to spare Jane and her family was a luxury that Mary could ill afford. Jane, in particular, posed a grave threat to the security of the state because as long as Henry's great-niece lived, she remained a figurehead for rebellion. After all, they pointed out, Mary's father had never hesitated to execute his potential rivals for the crown. The queen, however, clung to her principles. Her young cousin was the dupe of ruthless men who had manipulated her for their own ends, Mary maintained. "My conscience," she insisted, "will not permit me to have her put to death."[16]

Early Religious Reforms

Mary's advisers worried that the inexperienced monarch would prove as incautious in her religious policies as she had been in matters concerning her own security. They implored the queen to act slowly in her efforts to restore England to her beloved Catholicism. Because she had passed most of the last six years secluded in her country manors, Mary had lost touch with popular religious attitudes, they believed; she had no conception of how divided the English really were regarding Edward's Protestant reforms. During the course of Edward's reign, Protestantism had become deeply rooted in many parts of the realm, particularly in London and its surrounding counties. Yet Mary, her advisers suspected, had lulled herself into believing that most English Protestants had been bullied into accepting the new religion and would revert to the old faith now that a Catholic monarch sat on the throne.

Mary's advisers were particularly concerned that the queen might attempt to restore papal supremacy in England immediately. They realized that her new subjects had become accustomed to national control of the church. Even many English who detested the new prayer book and services would need some time to get used to the idea of an Italian pope interfering in their country's affairs again. Among the nobility, sentiment against a return to papal supremacy ran especially high. When Henry closed the kingdom's religious houses in the late 1530s, he parceled out thousands of acres of church land to his aristocratic supporters. They worried that once papal authority was reinstated, the Roman Catholic Church would want its valuable properties back.

After ruling as queen of England for only nine days, Lady Jane Grey was imprisoned in the Tower of London.

Mary never doubted that God had appointed her to bring England back into the Catholic fold. Nevertheless, she agreed to delay her God-given mission for a while longer. Until the time seemed ripe for a full return to Rome, Mary resolved to do all that she could to set her homeland on the correct spiritual path, however. During the autumn of 1553, she convinced Parliament to reinstate the Latin mass and repeal most of the Protestant legislation passed under Edward VI. At the queen's behest, Parliament also declared her mother and father's marriage valid and Mary herself legitimate.

A Husband for the Queen

During the first months of her reign, the issue of marriage preoccupied Mary almost as much as the issue of religious reform. As soon as she was proclaimed queen, people began to speculate on whom the new queen would wed. It was taken for granted that the first woman to rule England since Matilda's brief reign three centuries earlier needed a husband to protect and guide her. When Charles heard about Mary's accession, he immediately instructed Renard to "point out to her that it will be necessary, in order to be supported in the labor of governing and assisted in matters that are not of ladies' capacity, that she soon contract matrimony with the person who shall appear to her the most fit."[17] Should Mary desire his advice regarding her choice of husband, he would be happy to oblige, Charles assured the queen.

Mary herself was eager for a helpmate. She had never been taught to lead and felt out of her depth in the cutthroat world of court politics. For Mary, however, the most pressing reason to wed concerned the question of the royal succession. According to both the Act of Succession of 1544 and Henry's will, if Mary died child-less, the crown passed to Elizabeth, a prospect that deeply troubled the queen. Although Elizabeth diplo-matically attended mass whenever she was at court, Mary suspected that her sister remained a Protestant at heart. At thirty-seven years old, Mary feared that her childbearing years were nearly over. Determined to keep her sister off the throne, she was anxious to secure a suitable husband and produce a Catholic heir for England as quickly as possible.

As far as most of her English advisers and subjects were concerned, the best candidate for Mary's hand was a young man named Edward Courtenay. As the great-grandson of Edward IV, ruler of England during the late 1400s, Courtenay was the highest-ranking nobleman in the kingdom. Although Courtenay was a committed Catholic, even most Protestants favored him for the simple reason that he was an Englishman. If the queen married an outsider, people worried, he might treat the country as little more than a province of his homeland.

The Spanish Betrothal

Mary, however, was not interested in her compatriots' opinions regarding her marriage. She had decided to leave the selection of her husband entirely in the hands of her cousin Charles. "After God," she declared, "I desire to obey no one but the Emperor, whom I have always looked upon as a father. I am determined to follow His Majesty's advice and choose whomsoever he might recommend."[18] Like Mary, Charles V longed to see Catholicism restored in England. Even more, he wanted England to join Spain in a permanent military alliance against his homeland's archenemy, France. The best way to accomplish both of these objectives, the emperor believed, was to unite the English queen with the heir to the Spanish throne, his twenty-six-year-old son Philip, in matrimony.

Although the eleven-year age difference between her and Philip worried Mary, the queen found much to like about the proposed match. For one thing, the prince had a reputation as a passionate champion of orthodox Catholicism. For another, he was not only the son of the man whom Mary considered her greatest supporter but also the kinsman of her adored mother. Consequently, in late October the queen accepted Philip's proposal.

Mary's subjects were stunned by news of the betrothal. The English were notorious for their suspicion of outsiders, and there were no foreigners they distrusted more than the powerful and wealthy Spaniards. Spain's stranglehold over trade with the New World irked the English, and its brutal campaign against religious dissenters, the Inquisition, horrified them. Rumors that Philip intended to confiscate English lands and goods to pay for his homeland's numerous wars swept through the kingdom, and demonstrations against the marriage erupted in a number of cities and towns. Yet Mary refused to be swayed, even after Parliament sent a delegation to court to beg her to end the hated engagement. Her marriage, the queen huffily informed the delegates, was her own business and her mind was made up.

Wyatt's Rebellion

In January 1554, shortly after the marriage contract between Philip and Mary was finalized, English hostility toward the union erupted into rebellion. Centered in southern and central England, the uprising was organized by a small group of fiercely nationalistic gentlemen determined to block the Spanish marriage.

The insurrection, however, did not go according to plan. Four simultaneous uprisings were supposed to take

In 1554 Sir Thomas Wyatt (pictured) led a rebellion to protest Queen Mary's marriage plans to Philip of Spain.

place in southeastern, southwestern, and central England in the spring, before Philip arrived from Spain for the wedding. The rebellion's aristocratic leaders included Protestants like Jane Grey's father, the Duke of Suffolk, in the midlands and Catholics like Sir Thomas Wyatt in the southeast. After securing the major towns in their regions, the various rebel armies were to join forces and march to London to confront the queen directly. Unfortunately for the conspirators, Mary got wind of the plot early on and royal troops swiftly crushed the insurrections in both the midlands and the southwest.

The insurgents' hopes now rested on Wyatt, the most dynamic and determined of the rebel leaders. By the end of January, the charismatic knight had managed to raise a force of some fifteen thousand men in eastern

England, many of them deserters from the royal force sent from London to arrest him. In early February Wyatt and his followers boldly set out for the capital.

As Wyatt's army advanced on London, the queen's advisers pled with her to flee the city. Instead, she went to the Guildhall in the very heart of the capital to appeal directly to her subjects for their support. In a clear and deep voice that carried to the farthest reaches of the crowded hall, Mary reminded her audience that she was "the right and true inheritor of the crown of this realm of England." She would never do anything to harm her people or jeopardize England's independence, the queen said, for the good of the nation was her top priority: "I cannot tell how naturally the mother loveth the child for I was never the mother of any, but certainly if a prince and governor may as naturally and earnestly love her subjects, as the mother doth love the child, then assure yourselves that I, being your lady and mistress, do as earnestly love and favor you."[19]

"And now, good subjects," the queen concluded, "pluck up your hearts, and like true men, stand fast against these rebels, both our enemies and yours, and fear them not, for I assure you I fear them nothing at all!"[20] According to one witness, many of Mary's listeners wept openly at these words, and as she left the building, the hall reverberated with enthusiastic cries of "God save the queen."

Whatever misgivings they might have harbored regarding her choice of husband, as reports of Mary's rousing speech spread through the capital, thousands of Londoners loyally rushed to their courageous ruler's defense. On February 7, when Wyatt reached the city gates, his stunned troops were quickly surrounded and overwhelmed. Just as they had done six months earlier, the English people rallied behind King Henry's eldest daughter. Even so, the lesson that Mary drew from the events of February 1554 was a bitter one: If she was to fulfill her divine mission to return England to the one true church, she must ruthlessly eliminate anything—or anyone—who might attempt to get in the way of that goal.

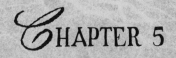

CHAPTER 5

TRAITORS AND HERETICS

Wyatt's Rebellion deeply hurt and angered Mary. The mercy she had shown her opponents at the beginning of her reign had been a mistake, she decided. In the future, she would not be as generous with those who threatened her crown or what she saw as her God-given mission: the restoration of Catholicism in England.

Severe Measures

Within days of Wyatt's surrender, London had become a city of corpses. At Mary's order, more than one hundred of the knight's followers were

Lady Jane Grey is beheaded on Tower Green in 1554.

hanged and their remains exhibited on gibbets at gathering places throughout the capital. The rotting bodies, the queen hoped, would serve as a powerful warning to other insurgents. Wyatt himself was hanged, drawn, and quartered before a large crowd on Tower Hill. For months after the gruesome execution, the rebel leader's severed limbs adorned the city gates.

Several of England's highest-ranking nobles also perished as a result of the uprising. The Duke of Suffolk, pardoned just six months earlier for his role in Northumberland's plot, was beheaded for conspiring with Wyatt. An even more prominent casualty of the revolt was Suffolk's daughter, Jane. At first Mary had hesitated to sign her cousin's death warrant. The imprisoned teen could not possibly have had any knowledge of the conspiracy, she realized. The queen's advisers, however, insisted that the young woman who had once worn Mary's crown must die: Innocent or not, Jane was an obvious rallying point for the queen's growing number of opponents. Charles V was particularly adamant regarding this point. Until Mary's dangerous relative was eliminated, he would not allow his son to go to England, the emperor declared. Because her marriage to Philip was an essential part of her plan to rebuild English Catholicism, Mary felt she had little choice but to yield to Charles's demands, and on February 12 Jane and Guildford Dudley were beheaded on the Tower Green.

Mary's decision to execute Jane was heavily influenced by Charles V, shown in this painting.

With Jane out of the picture, Mary focused her attention on another potential figurehead for her enemies: Elizabeth Tudor. Charles's ambassador, Simon Renard, was convinced that the twenty-year-old was as serious a threat to Mary as Jane had been. He even suspected that Wyatt had planned to overthrow Mary in Elizabeth's favor. Although Elizabeth denied any knowledge of Wyatt's alleged plot to place her on the throne, at Renard's urging Mary had her sibling imprisoned in the Tower of London. Elizabeth languished in the London stronghold for two months before the queen concluded there was no solid evidence against her. Renard was dismayed by Elizabeth's release from the Tower, but the queen was immovable. Mary felt little affection for the daughter of her mother's great enemy, Anne Boleyn. Nonetheless, her conscience would not permit her to treat her own sister unjustly.

A Time of Hope and Joy

On July 25, 1554, Mary wed Philip of Spain in a magnificent ceremony. So began what many historians believe to have been the happiest period of the queen's adult life.

Married life clearly agreed with the thirty-seven-year-old queen, who was enchanted by her refined and pious bridegroom. "I daily discover in my husband . . . so many virtues and perfections that I constantly pray God to grant me grace to please him,"[21] Mary wrote to her father-in-law, the emperor, in August. Two months later the queen joyfully announced that she was pregnant. Mary had always believed that her marriage to Philip was God's will, and her pregnancy seemed to confirm that view. Now England would have a Catholic heir to preserve the true faith after she was gone.

Parliament's willingness to finally repeal Henry VIII's Act of Supremacy and reunite England to Rome added greatly to Mary's happiness during the fall of 1554. On November 30 Cardinal Reginald Pole, the new papal legate (representative) to England, formally received the submission of the realm and its rulers to the authority of Pope Julius III. Mary's success in persuading Parliament to reestablish papal supremacy was closely linked to Julius's stand regarding former church property in the kingdom. In his eagerness to return England to the Catholic fold after twenty years of separation, Julius promised to relinquish all claims to the valuable lands obtained by Henry VIII's supporters when the king dissolved the monasteries and convents.

Mary's Campaign Against the Heretics Begins

By the end of 1554, Mary had also convinced Parliament to reinstate several old heresy acts that had

In exchange for papal control of England, Pope Julius III surrendered his claims to recover church property that Henry VIII had confiscated.

been repealed under Edward. The laws empowered bishops and other high-ranking religious officials to try suspected heretics in special church courts. Any heretic who refused to renounce his or her unorthodox views was to be turned over to the local sheriff for execution. According to the acts, condemned heretics were to suffer a particularly cruel form of punishment: They were to be tied to a stake and burned alive.

Mary regarded the revival of the brutal laws as a crucial part of her crusade to replant Catholicism in England. Convinced that most Protestants had converted for political reasons and would quickly return to the old faith following her accession, the new queen had tried to be patient with the religious dissenters in her realm. By the end of

1554, however, Mary's patience with the heretics had run out. Mary had ruled for more than a year. Yet encouraged by a large underground of preachers and organizers, Protestantism still flourished in many parts of the kingdom. Now that the country was officially reconciled to Rome, the queen was determined to end the heretics' harmful influence once and for all. Mary did not expect to have to burn many dissenters; Protestantism would swiftly die out once she had eliminated its top leadership, she believed.

The first heresy trials of Mary's reign took place in January 1555, and by February the burnings had begun. All the queen's earliest victims were well-known figures within the Protestant community. Three popular preachers were the first to perish: John Rogers in Smithfield, Lawrence Saunders in Coventry, and Rowland Taylor in Hadleigh. Next to die were two prominent Protestant bishops: John Hooper, who suffered an especially slow and painful death at the stake in Gloucester, and Robert Ferrar, who was burned in Carmarthen before a large and sympathetic crowd in March. Mary was surprised but not particularly concerned by the widespread popular outcry against the brutal executions; she had absolute faith both in the rightness of her cause and in its ultimate success.

A Bitter Disappointment

Soon after Ferrar's execution, the queen retreated into her private quarters to await the birth of her child and heir. A cradle was prepared and nurses appointed. Yet Mary's due date came and went and the royal cradle remained empty. By early summer, it was evident that Mary had either miscarried or never been pregnant in the first place. Some historians now believe that the physical symptoms the queen displayed during the months when she believed herself pregnant, including cessation of her menstrual periods and abdominal swelling, were actually early signs of cancer of the uterus or ovaries.

The realization that there was no baby was a terrible blow for Mary. Her depression deepened when her adored husband left England for Europe in August on what he claimed was urgent business for his father. Philip insisted that he would only be gone a few weeks, but Mary was not deceived. She knew that her husband was restless and unhappy in his adopted country. According to the terms of their marriage contract, although he was called king of England, Philip possessed no real authority over the realm. Thanks to the efforts of the nationalistic English officials who wrote the agreement, Mary's Spanish husband was not supposed to make any appointments to state or church offices or interfere in the country's policies. It was common knowledge that Philip had only signed the humiliating contract to please his father.

While Philip was unfailingly courteous toward his wife, for him the marriage was strictly a political alliance. When he departed England in August 1555, Philip

Protestants are burned at the stake in a square in London. Many English citizens were shocked by these barbaric executions.

promised to return as quickly as possible, but some new crisis in Charles's domains that required his attention always seemed to crop up. As weeks lengthened into months, Mary wrote one tearful letter after another to Philip imploring him to come home. Then, in January 1556, an ailing Charles V decided to relinquish his throne and Philip became ruler of Spain, the Netherlands, and Spain's possessions in Italy and the Americas. (The title of Holy Roman Emperor, however, was awarded to Charles's brother Ferdinand.) Now, even if he had wished to, Philip was in no position to return to England anytime soon.

The Burnings Continue

Even Mary's preoccupation with her absent spouse could not distract her from what she considered as her religious duty. By mid-1556, England's Protestant leadership had been all but wiped out. Those Protestant clerics who had not fled the country had been executed, including three of the most influential churchmen under Henry and Edward, bishops Hugh Latimer and Nicholas Ridley and Archbishop Thomas Cranmer. Yet the loss of their top leaders had failed to discourage the Protestants; if anything, the unwavering courage and faith that Ridley, Cranmer, and Mary's other prominent victims displayed in the face of death united and emboldened the dissenters as never before. Grimly determined to bring her misguided subjects to their senses, the queen decided to expand her antiheresy crusade to include the Protestant rank and file. Hundreds of ordinary men and women—shopkeepers and teachers, farmers and fishermen, weavers and house-wives—were imprisoned and tried for their unorthodox views. Inspired by their martyred leaders, many of the accused chose to perish at the stake rather than renounce their faith.

As Mary's war against the Protestants intensified, so too did public outcry against the horrific executions. The burnings invariably attracted large crowds, and those who witnessed the victims' agonizing deaths were forever haunted by what they had seen. Reports of the martyrs' remarkable devotion and suffering soon spread through the realm. People spoke in hushed tones of the preacher who prayed for his killers as they lit the rushes beneath him, the humble laborer who sang hymns until his lips were completely burned away, and the young blind woman who had to be led to the stake by her weeping brother. Stories were also told of the many victims whose agony was unnecessarily prolonged because their incompetent executioners used rushes that

THE MARTYRDOM OF THOMAS CRANMER

There was no heretic whom Mary was more eager to bring to justice than Thomas Cranmer, the archbishop of Canterbury. Mary detested Cranmer not only as the author of the Protestant Book of Common Prayer but also as the person who had officially annulled her mother's marriage and made her illegitimate in the eyes of the law. Determined to force a recantation from the elderly archbishop, Mary had Cranmer interrogated, humiliated, and bullied. He was even compelled to watch his close friends, bishops Hugh Latimer and Nicholas Ridley, die at the stake. Finally, in February 1556, a few days after he was informed that the queen had given him up as beyond redemption and signed his death warrant, Cranmer broke.

Over the course of the next few weeks, Cranmer wrote several recantations. In them, he renounced the Protestant beliefs he had championed over the last two decades and humbly begged the queen's forgiveness. Nonetheless, Mary would not relent. Cranmer was a liar and a fraud, Mary declared, and the execution would go forward as planned.

Once Cranmer realized that he must die, he withdrew all his recantations and proclaimed himself a convinced Protestant. When he was taken to Oxford to be burned on March 21, 1556, at the exact site where Ridley and Latimer had died six months earlier, Cranmer pledged that his right hand would be the first part of him to burn because it had signed the hated recantations. True to his word, after the fire was lit Cranmer immediately thrust his hand into the flames and kept it there until it was burned to ashes. Cranmer never made a sound during his terrible ordeal, and his dignity and courage made a deep impression on the large crowd that had gathered to watch the execution.

A few days after Cranmer's death, Mary ordered that the archbishop's recantations be published. If she had hoped to put Cranmer in a bad light by releasing the documents, her scheme completely backfired. Most people were more interested in Cranmer's dramatic words and actions on the day of his execution than in his earlier recantations. Some Protestants even declared that the recantations were a hoax and denounced the queen as a coldhearted liar.

were too damp or wood that was too green to burn quickly. Even many English who disdained Protestant teachings were repulsed by the killings.

Alarmed by the depth of popular feeling against the executions, many of Mary's advisers, including her staunchly Catholic chancellor, Stephen Gardiner, pleaded with her to halt the burnings. Even Philip, who viciously persecuted heretics in Spain and the Netherlands, worried that Mary's violent crusade was a mistake. Although most English assumed that Philip supported his wife's bloody campaign, the king quietly urged Mary to abandon the controversial executions. Like Gardiner, Philip realized that the killings had failed to frighten the Protestants into submission as Mary had hoped. Instead, they had merely served to make the queen's subjects more distrustful of her than ever.

As opposition to her savage crusade both within and outside of the government grew, Mary's attitude toward the heretics hardened. Convinced that it was her Christian duty to protect her realm against the dangers of false doctrine by whatever means necessary, Mary vowed to take an even harsher line with the dissenters. She rebuked one local official because he had spared the life of a man who recanted moments before his execution and scolded the bishop of London for his slowness in bringing suspected heretics to trial. She also ordered that more guards be present at the executions to arrest any spectators "who shall misuse themselves either by comforting, aiding or praising the offenders or otherwise use themselves to the ill example of others."[22]

A Host of Setbacks

In March 1557, as Mary's bloody campaign against the heretics escalated, Philip sailed back to England after an absence of more than eighteen months. The queen's joy at his return, however, proved short-lived, for Philip had come back not out of affection for his wife but merely to obtain her assistance in Spain's newest conflict with France. Once he had persuaded Mary to declare war on his homeland's old enemy, the king departed abruptly for Europe. For Mary, insult was added to injury when the new pope, Paul IV, a staunch ally of the French king, recalled his legate, the queen's close adviser, Reginald Pole, in retaliation for her support of Spain.

Soon after Pole's dismissal, Mary received another serious blow when Calais, England's last toehold on the continent, fell to a French army. A thriving seaport on France's northwestern coast, Calais had been under English control for more than two centuries. When the French besieged the city in January 1558, the English garrisons were taken by surprise and swiftly overwhelmed. Mary's subjects were dismayed by news of the humiliating defeat, which they blamed chiefly on the queen. If Mary had not dragged the kingdom into her Spanish husband's war, Calais would still be in English hands, they grumbled. In the wake of the loss of Calais, public dissatisfaction with Mary's reign was greater than ever before.

During the winter of 1558, the forty-two-year-old queen found consolation for the debacle at Calais in the belief that she was pregnant. It was a conviction that few others shared. In light of the queen's age and past medical history, most people at court attributed her swollen belly to illness rather than impending motherhood. Mary had calculated a due date of late March. When June arrived and the royal nursery was still empty, the queen at last faced the truth: There would be no baby for her to love and no Catholic heir for England.

The Death of a Queen

Mary's health steadily worsened during the summer of 1558. By autumn she had begun to drift in and out of consciousness. In her lucid moments, the queen grieved for the shameful loss of Calais. "When I am dead and opened," she told one of her servants, "you shall find Calais lying in my heart."[23]

Aware that Mary's days were numbered, the queen's advisers begged her to name Elizabeth Tudor as her heir. (According to the terms of Mary and Philip's marital contract, Philip had no claim to the English throne should he outlive his wife.) The twenty-five-year-old princess was unquestionably Mary's legal successor: Both the Act of Succession of 1544 and Henry's will designated Elizabeth as next in line after her sister should Mary die childless. Even so, determined to ensure a peaceful succession, Mary's councilors wanted the queen to formally endorse Elizabeth. Fearful that Elizabeth was a secret Protestant, Mary resisted her councilors' pleas for weeks. On November 7, however, the queen finally accepted the inevitable and proclaimed her support for her sibling. At the same time, however, she admonished Elizabeth to preserve the old religion in England.

Ten days later, on the morning of November 17, 1558, Mary died at St. James Palace in London, probably from cancer of the ovaries or uterus. According to her lady-in-waiting Jane Dormer, shortly before her death Mary consoled her weeping attendants by telling them "what good dreams she had, seeing many little children like angels playing before her, . . . giving her more than earthly comfort."[24]

Mary's Legacy

When Mary's death was announced in London, foreign visitors were shocked by the response in the streets of

the capital. Few people appeared to mourn for their departed monarch. Instead, Londoners devoted themselves to joyfully welcoming Mary's successor. All over the city church bells rang out, bonfires were lit, and people "did eat and drink and made merry for the new Queen Elizabeth,"[25] noted one observer. Mary Tudor had ascended the throne on a wave of popular enthusiasm. Just five years later it was painfully evident that her subjects were all too happy to be rid of her.

Mary's widespread unpopularity at the end of her reign had many causes. The Spanish marriage, the loss of Calais, and the high financial cost of the war against France had all contributed

In 1558 Mary's half sister Elizabeth, a devout Protestant, ascended the throne.

JOHN FOXE AND HIS FAMOUS BOOK OF MARTYRS

That Mary's executions were still remembered and reviled by the English centuries after her death owes much to the sixteenth-century university professor and minister John Foxe. Foxe, a staunch Protestant, fled England for Switzerland soon after Mary was crowned. When reports of the burnings reached him in Basle, Foxe was horrified. Motivated by indignation at his government's cruelty as well as by religious zeal, Foxe decided to write a detailed account of Mary I's Protestant martyrs.

First published in England five years after Mary's death under the title *Actes and Monuments of these Latter and Perillous Dayes*, Foxe's chronicle of the nearly three hundred men and women burned to death during Mary's reign soon became popularly known as Foxe's *Book of Martyrs*. Under Elizabeth's new Protestant regime, Foxe's tear-wrenching and often grisly account of Mary's martyrs quickly became a best seller. Elizabeth herself was such an avid admirer of Foxe's work that she ordered a copy of the Book of Martyrs to be placed in every church in the kingdom so that all of her subjects might have the opportunity to study it.

One of the most frequently reprinted books in the English language, Foxe's Book of Martyrs remained a best seller in Foxe's homeland until well into the nineteenth century. Although Foxe never used the nickname "Bloody Mary" in his work—that epithet for Mary was coined in the seventeenth century—for centuries after her death his famous book helped to fix an image of her in the minds of the English people as a coldhearted and violent persecutor of martyrs.

Foxe's Book of Martyrs *was illustrated with engravings like this one, showing the burning of an ordinary woman.*

to the growing public dissatisfaction with Mary during her brief rule. Without doubt, Mary's violent crusade against the Protestant heretics was also a critical factor in her fall from grace. Although her predecessors had executed heretics, too, the scale of the killings under Mary was unique in English history. Henry VII burned 10 heretics in twenty-four years; Henry VIII burned 80 heretics in just under forty years. In stark contrast, during a period of not quite four years, lasting from February 1555 until November 1558, some 230 men and 60 women were burned in England for their religious views. Even in an era accustomed to violence and public executions, Mary's subjects were appalled by the sheer scope of her brutal persecution.

Historians agree that far from strengthening English Catholicism, Mary's bloody campaign against the Protestant heretics nearly destroyed it. On the very day of her accession, Elizabeth I put a halt to the hated burnings. By 1559 Protestantism had once again become England's state religion after Parliament, with Elizabeth's blessing, passed legislation that made the queen head of the English church and Cranmer's Protestant prayer book again the basis for all religious services. Catholicism had become so discredited under Mary's unpopular reign that the vast majority of

Elizabeth's subjects quietly accepted the reforms. Over the years, memories of Mary's savage persecutions continued to dog the Catholic cause in which she had believed so fervently. Even as late as the nineteenth century, many English still associated Catholicism with violence and tyranny, and Catholics remained a tiny and oppressed minority within the kingdom. The queen who had hoped to go down in history as the savior of English Catholicism was instead remembered as Bloody Mary, the individual who, more than any other, had ensured the triumph of Protestant Christianity in England.

CHRONOLOGY

1509	King Henry VIII marries his brother Arthur's widow, Catherine of Aragon.
1516	Mary Tudor is born to Henry and Catherine on February 18.
1533	Henry has his marriage to Catherine annulled by Archbishop Cranmer; Elizabeth, the daughter of Anne Boleyn and Henry, is born.
1534	The Act of Succession makes Henry and Anne Boleyn's children heirs to the throne; the Act of Supremacy makes Henry the supreme head of the Church of England.
1536	Catherine of Aragon dies; Anne Boleyn is executed, and Henry marries Jane Seymour.
1537	Edward, the son of Henry and Jane Seymour, is born.
1543	Henry marries his sixth wife, Catherine Parr.
1544	A parliamentary act reinstates Mary in the succession after Edward and his heirs.

1547	Henry dies and Edward VI is crowned.
1549	The Act of Uniformity bans Catholic mass in England.
1553	A dying Edward names his Protestant cousin Jane Grey as his successor; Edward dies on July 6 and Grey is crowned four days later; Mary marches on London and secures the throne, ending Grey's nine-day reign.
1554	The Wyatt Rebellion is crushed; Mary weds Prince Philip of Spain; England is brought back under papal authority, and old heresy laws are revived.
1555	Executions of Protestant heretics begin.
1558	England loses the port city of Calais in its war with France; Mary dies on November 17 at age 42; her half sister, Elizabeth, becomes queen.

GLOSSARY

annulment A ruling that a marriage was never a lawful union in the eyes of the church.

betrothal A formal pledge to marry.

bishop A senior Christian clergyman who is responsible for the administration and spiritual life of a certain diocese or region; an archbishop is a bishop of the highest rank.

cardinal A high official in the Roman Catholic Church appointed by the pope and standing just below him in rank.

Church of England The national Protestant church founded in 1534 by King Henry VIII when he renounced the authority of the pope over English Christians.

dowry Money, land, or goods presented to the groom or his family by the bride's family at the time of the marriage.

duke A British nobleman whose rank is directly below that of a prince.

gibbet A gallows with a projecting arm for suspending and exhibiting the corpses of lawbreakers after hanging.

heresy A belief that differs from traditional or established religious teaching.

lute A stringed instrument similar to a guitar.

Parliament England's national legislative body.

Protestantism A religious movement opposing Roman Catholicism that originated in the early sixteenth century and grew to include many churches and denominations believing in salvation by faith alone and denying the authority of the pope.

Reformation The religious movement launched in western Europe in the early 1500s that sought to reform some of the practices and doctrines of the Roman Catholic Church; it eventually led to the creation of Protestant churches.

Roman Catholic Church The Christian church whose supreme head is the pope.

Tudor dynasty The ruling family of England from 1485, when Mary I's grandfather, Henry VII, seized power, until 1603, when Mary's half sister and successor, Elizabeth I, died.

virginal A small keyboard instrument popular in the sixteenth and seventeenth centuries.

Source Notes

Introduction: "Bloody Mary"

1. Quoted in John Foxe, *Foxe's Book of Martyrs,* ed. W. Grinton Berry. Grand Rapids, MI: Baker Book House, 1989, p. 309.

2. Quoted in Foxe, *Foxe's Book of Martyrs,* p. 310.

Chapter 1: The Young Princess

3. Quoted in David Loades, *Mary Tudor: A Life.* Oxford: Basil Blackwell, 1989, p. 14.

4. Carolly Erickson, *Bloody Mary.* New York: St. Martin's Griffin, 1978, p. 38.

5. Erickson, *Bloody Mary,* p. 88.

Chapter 2: "The Most Unhappy Lady in Christendom"

6. Quoted in H.F.M. Prescott, *Mary Tudor: The Spanish Tudor.* London: Eyre & Spottiswoode, 1952, p. 57.

7. Quoted in Erickson, *Bloody Mary,* p. 113.

8. Quoted in Erickson, *Bloody Mary,* p. 104.

9. Quoted in David Loades, *The Reign of Mary Tudor: Politics, Government & Religion in England, 1553–58.* New York: Longman, 1979, p. 10.

Chapter 3: Mary's Changing Fortunes

10. Quoted in Alison Weir, *The Children of Henry VIII.* New York: Ballantine, 1996, p. 118.

11. Alison Plowden, *Lady Jane Grey: Nine Days Queen.* Gloucestershire, UK: Sutton, 2003, p. 70.

12. Quoted in Plowden, *Lady Jane Grey,* p. 70.

Chapter 4: The New Queen

13. Quoted in Weir, *The Children of Henry VIII,* p. 165.

14. Quoted in Plowden, *Lady Jane Grey,* p. 103.

15. Quoted in Alison Plowden, *Tudor Women: Queens and Commoners.* Gloucestershire, UK: Sutton, 1998, p. 134.

16. Quoted in Prescott, *Mary Tudor,* p. 234.

17. Quoted in Weir, *The Children of Henry VIII,* p. 183.

18. Quoted in Weir, *The Children of Henry VIII,* p. 187.

19. Quoted in Erickson, *Bloody Mary,* pp. 353–54.

20. Quoted in Erickson, *Bloody Mary*, p. 354.

Chapter 5: Traitors and Heretics

21. Quoted in Loades, *The Reign of Mary Tudor*, p. 157.

22. Quoted in Jasper Ridley, *Bloody Mary's Martyrs: The Story of*

England's Terror. New York: Caroll & Graf, 2001, p. 143.

23. Quoted in Prescott, *Mary Tudor*, p. 474.

24. Quoted in Erickson, *Bloody Mary*, p. 481.

25. Quoted in Erickson, *Bloody Mary*, p. 481.

FOR MORE INFORMATION

Books

Marilyn Tower Oliver, *Henry VIII*. San Diego: Lucent, 2004.

Freda Roll, *Mary I: The History of an Unhappy Tudor Queen*. Englewood Cliffs, NJ: Prentice-Hall, 1980.

Jessica Saraga, *Tudor Monarchs*. London: Batsford, 1992.

——— *What Life Was Like in the Realm of Elizabeth: England, AD1533-1603*. Alexandria, VA: Time-Life, 1998.

Richard Worth, *Henry the VIII and the Reformation in World History*. Berkeley Heights, NJ: Enslow, 2001.

Web Sites

Mary I (www.tudorhistory.org/mary). This site includes a detailed account of Mary I's life and reign, a portrait gallery, and a play about Mary by Alfred Lord Tennyson.

Mary Tudor (http://home.earthlink.net/~elisale). This site includes a biography of Mary I, a replica of her wedding dress, and a family tree.

Tudor England (http://englishhistory.net/tudor.html). This site includes useful articles on Mary I, Elizabeth I, Henry VIII, and Lady Jane Grey.

INDEX

Act of Succession, 35, 37, 50, 63, 64, 77, 98, 103

Act of Supremacy, 36, 37, 87, 103

Act of Uniformity, 56–62, 63, 104

adultery, 48, 53

Anne of Cleves, 48, 53

annulment, 25–27, 30–31, 41, 48, 103

Boleyn, Anne, 42, 53, 86
  children of, 32, 38, 40
  death of, 39, 41, 103
  as Henry VIII's mistress, 24, 27
  marries Henry VIII, 31
  Mary I and, 33–34
Book of Common Prayer, 56–57, 94
Book of Martyrs, 100
burnings, 6–7, 9, 88, 89, 92–93, 95–96

Calais, 96–97
Catherine of Aragon, 11, 14–15, 17, 36, 42
  annulment of marriage of, 30–31, 103
  death of, 38, 103
  marriage of, to Henry VIII, 24–27
  Oath of Supremacy and, 37–38
  relationship with Mary I, 20, 27–29
Catholic Church, 7, 8, 20, 25, 35, 45–46, 52, 54, 56
  Charles V and, 78

Mary I and, 29, 63, 101–2
return of, to England, 74–76, 88–89
Chapuys, Eustace, 34, 35, 43, 44
Charles V, 16–17, 22, 26, 58–59, 60, 72, 76, 78, 85
  relinquishes throne, 92
Church of England, 5, 36, 42, 55, 56, 103
Clement VII (pope), 25–27, 30, 35
Courtenay, Edward, 77
Cranmer, Thomas, 30–31, 41, 55–56, 64, 92, 94, 103

dauphin, 15
"Defender of the Faith," 55
dowry, 16–17, 22
Dudley, Guildford, 64, 72, 85
Dudley, John. See
  Northumberland, Duke of

Edward VI, 7, 50
  becomes king, 51–52, 104
  birth of, 44–45, 103
  death of, 66–67
  disinherits his sisters, 64
  guardian of, 59
  health of, 63
  Mary I and, 60–62
  Protestantism and, 55
  successor of, 63, 64
Elizabeth I
  becomes queen, 99, 101, 104
  birth of, 32–33
  as heir to throne, 35, 49–50, 64, 77, 86, 98

executions, 8–9, 37, 39, 48, 72, 84–85, 88, 89, 93, 101, 104

Ferdinand (king), 14–15
Ferrar, Robert, 89
Fisher, John, 37
Foxe, John, 100
France, 15, 17, 22–23, 78, 96
Francis I, 15, 22–23, 28

Gardiner, Stephen, 72, 95
Greenwich Palace, 15, 22, 66
Grey, Lady Jane, 63–65, 71, 84–85, 104
  charged with treason, 72
  Mary I and, 73–74
  as queen, 67–69

heir, to throne, 12–13, 32, 45, 77, 98, 103

Henry VII, 14–15, 101
Henry VIII, 8, 11–14, 15, 20–21, 22
  Anne Boleyn and, 27, 31, 35, 41
  annulment of marriage, 25–27, 30–31, 41, 48, 103
  Catherine Howard and, 53
  Catherine of Aragon and, 24–27, 29, 103
  death of, 50–51, 104
  as "Defender of the Faith," 55
  executions by, 101
  health of, 50
  Jane Seymour and, 40–42
  shuts monasteries and

110

convents, 45–46
wives of, 41–42, 48, 49
heresy, 6, 8, 87–89, 95, 101
Hooper, John, 89
Howard, Catherine, 48, 53

illegitimacy, 28, 31, 35, 42, 43, 50, 76, 94
Isabella (princess), 22
Italy, 26

Julius III (pope), 87

Latimer, Hugh, 5–6, 92, 94
Leo X (pope), 55
Ludlow Castle, 21, 22
Luther, Martin, 52, 54, 55

martyrs, 9, 93, 100
Mary I, 7
  Act of Succession and, 37
  Act of Uniformity and, 57–62
  advisers of, 72–73
  becomes queen, 71–74
  campaigns against heretics, 87–89
  Catherine Parr and, 49
  Catholicism and, 29, 63, 101
  childhood of, 11–23
  death of, 97–98, 104
  declared Princess of Wales, 21–23
  education of, 17–18
  Edward VI and, 51, 60–62, 63
  Elizabeth I and, 33
  health of, 34–38, 97–98
  illegitimacy and, 28, 31, 35, 42, 43, 50, 76, 94
  Jane Seymour and, 44–45
  legacy of, 99, 101–102
  letter of submission and,

43–44
  marriage of, 76–79, 86–87
  parents' marriage annulment and, 31–32, 47
  Protestantism and, 55–59
  reaction of, to Queen Jane, 69–71
  relationship with Henry VIII, 20–21, 32, 42–43, 48–49
  relationship with mother, 20, 27–29, 32, 38
  religious reforms of, 74–76
  teen years of, 27–29
  war against Protestantism and, 93
  Wyatt's rebellion and, 79–82, 83–84
monarchs, 13, 36
More, Sir Thomas, 36–37

Ninety-five Theses, 52, 54, 55
Northumberland, Duke of, 59–62, 63, 64, 84
  Edward VI's death and, 67–69, 71
  execution of, 72

Oath of Supremacy, 36

papal supremacy, 36, 42, 45, 75, 87, 104
Parr, Catherine, 49, 103
Paul IV (pope), 96
Philip of Spain, 78–79, 85, 86–87, 90–92, 95, 96, 98, 104
Pole, Reginald, 96
Princess of Wales, 21–23, 32–33
princesses, 14
Protestantism, 5, 6, 7, 8, 52, 54–59, 64, 92–93, 95–96

after Edward VI's death, 74–76
  as England's religion, 101
  Mary I and, 88–89

queens, 12, 13

Reformation, 52
Renard, Simon, 72, 76, 86
Ridley, Nicholas, 5–6, 92, 94
Rogers, John, 89
Roman Catholic Church. See Catholic Church

Saunders, Lawrence, 89
Seymour, Edward. See Somerset, Duke of
Seymour, Jane, 40–42, 44–45, 103
Shelton, Lady, 34
Somerset, Duke of, 52, 55, 57, 58–59
Spain, 16, 17, 78, 79, 96
succession, royal, 13, 49–50, 77, 103
  see also Act of Succession
Suffolk, Duke of, 72, 80, 84

Taylor, Rowland, 89
Tower of London, 39, 41, 71, 86
treason, 36, 39, 43, 53, 57, 72
Tudor, Arthur, 14–15
Tudor, Elizabeth. See Elizabeth I
Tudor, Henry. See Henry VIII

Vives, Luis, 17, 18

witchcraft, 40
women, 12–13
Wyatt, Thomas, 79–82, 83–84, 86, 104

INDEX

PICTURE CREDITS